The Pastor's Prospective and Pronouncement

It came even to pass, as the trumpeters and singers were as one, to make one sound to be heard in praising and thanking the Lord; and when they lifted up their voice with the trumpets and cymbals and instruments of musick, and praised the Lord, saying, For he is good; for his mercy endureth for ever: that then the house was filled with a cloud, even the house of the Lord; So that the priests could not stand to minister by reason of the the cloud: for the glory of the Lord had filled the house of God. 2 Chronicles 5:13,14

The divinely inspired prototype for a music minister is enveloped throughout diverse biblical experiences found in the Holy Writ, which must dictate and direct our secular course and spiritual composition. The chronicles of those ambassadors anointed to infuse the atmosphere with empowering musical arpeggios and ensconcing scriptural hegemonies have historically encircled experiences that infused and inculcated a dependency on God. The trails and testimonies of these compos mentis disciples are litanies that demonstrate the glory of the Lord, proclaim the holiness of His acts, and celebrate His majesty through impressive genres of religious musical compositions and lyrics. This declaration is clearly evidenced through the extraordinary and impressive witness of our Minister of Music, Evangelist Valerie Daniels-Carter.

Valerie Daniels-Carter's unfeigned fidelity to ministry excellence exemplifies an unparallel archetype and epitomizes an emblematic prominence afforded only to the divinely commissioned. Her biblical based integrity, business acumen, stellar moral fiber, charming elegance, astounding insightfulness, and exemplary demeanor are distinctive foundational values consistently demonstrated throughout her persona, which were intentionally instilled by her parents John W. Daniels and Supervisor Kathryn Daniels and grandparents Reverend G.T. and Inez Townsel. Countless thousands have globally celebrated her notoriety as a prolific composer, enterprising entrepreneur, and philanthropic personality. We applaud those notable accomplishments, but esteem her Pentecostal witness and sagacity. Her musical credits are numerous as a composer, musician, directress, and producer in the gospel music industry. She has ascended from a young urban girl interested in piano, drums, and various string and wind instruments to a noted regional Minister of Music assigned by the legendary Dr. Mattie Moss-Clark and owner of her own publishing and distribution company.

Although her eminence engenders recognition as one of America's largest franchisee entrepreneurs, we pause to endorse the presence of the Lord embodied in her profound ministry that fills our sanctuary, ameliorates our ministries, and enhances our lives as a direct result of her phenomenal spiritual embrace executed in our ministry.

Bishop Sedgwick Daniels, Establishmentarian/Minister

"There is nothing too hard for God!"

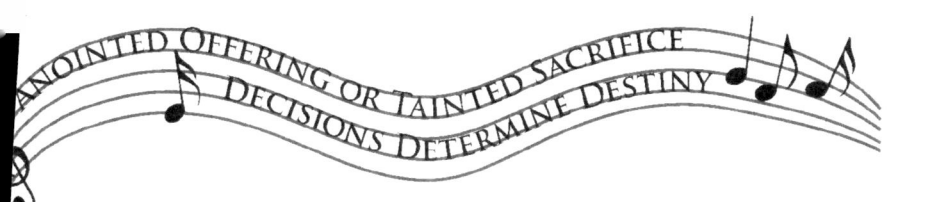

Anointed Offering or Tainted Sacrifice — Decisions Determine Destiny

INTRODUCTION

It is substantiated through the Word of God that we are wonderfully made. When God gifted you as a music minister, He did so with intent in mind. We must continuously examine our motives as they relate to, *how, what* and *when* we do what we do. The path we take is not just about us, it is also about the lives we will influence. I get excited when I see an effective and anointed music minister operating within their calling. It is true that gifts and callings come without repentance. Therefore, an individual who is gifted in the arts has a choice relative to whom and where they elect to serve. I believe when an artist knows and understands who they are, why they have been gifted and who has gifted them, they should honor the giver of the gift and operate within the boundaries and territory that have been established by the author and finisher of our faith.

Operating within your calling is a choice you make. Even though God has a divine purpose for your life, He never forces you to select a certain direction. I can only offer wise and godly counsel, but the final decision is yours to make. The insights in this book are lessons I have garnered while serving in music ministry. When you read this book in the spirit in which it has been penned, I pray you are blessed and gain insight. I have pursued music excellence and sought the mind of God concerning it for over 40

Anointed Offering or Tainted Sacrifice — Decisions Determine Destiny

years. While on this journey, I have experienced many things which have earned me the right to make sound arguments for purpose-driven music ministers, while challenging what appears to be a rapidly degrading influential norm. There were many influential persons who assisted me through my musical journey. It is now time I share my insights and experience with other music ministers.

Music is a universal language. It transcends cultures, ethnicities, geographical boundaries, gender, age, economic status and religion. From birth until death, music is intertwined in our lives. When we are born, there is an expression of joyful sounds, and once we transition from earth to life eternal, there is suppuration. Music is everlasting; we are assured by scriptures that music will be an ongoing activity in heaven (Isaiah 51:11). Music, whether instrumental or vocal, is an enriching expression of tones. It is used to celebrate, heal and comfort. Music is an emotional expression of song, instrumentation or dance which is celebrated by all cultures around the world. God in His wisdom and providence created a means of expression called *music* to praise and worship Him, edify the believer and unify the world.

Praise is an expression to God for His worth. We thank Him for being our great creator and comforter. Praise is common among believers. The inward attitude of praise is expressed through an

ANOINTED OFFERING OR TAINTED SACRIFICE
DECISIONS DETERMINE DESTINY

outward emotion. I believe it is impossible to praise God and be depressed at the same time. The moment you enter the realm of praise, your entire spirit is lifted; your act of speaking appreciation and thanksgiving to God releases positive energy. Praise is an expression of sharing with others just how wonderful God is. Psalms 9:1 states, "*I will praise thee, O LORD, with my whole heart; I will shew forth all thy marvelous works.*"

Worship means to honor, give homage and reverence. Worship takes on a posture of humbleness. We worship in spirit and in truth with a reverential attitude of mind and body. Worship leads us into the presence of God and we give deference and admiration to Him for who He is. We bow our heads in adoration and veneration to His presence, and we are awed by His visitation. Our spiritual emotions and total being are unrestricted as we esteem and offer great affection to the *Great I AM*. To worship God is to love Him.

Edification is the art of building. It is our responsibility to edify one another. The Bible states in I Thessalonians 5:11, "*Wherefore comfort yourselves together, and edify one another, even as also ye do.*" In the early church, believers often included opportunity for mutual edification among themselves. This encouragement was not just for a moment in time, but the edification also encircled their hope in Christ's return. They were

ANOINTED OFFERING OR TAINTED SACRIFICE DECISIONS DETERMINE DESTINY

taught to continuously keep His return in the forefront of their fellowship and when they assembled. How different would our musical presentation be if before every performance we were reminded that Christ may return today and this is your final recital to show Him how much you love Him? I believe too many musicians and singers lack this level of consciousness. We are too causal in our presentation and we do not fully comprehend the potency of an anointed music calling. When music is ministered properly, it is the catalyst that ushers in praise and worship. Music is a powerful gift to the Body of Christ. The enemy recognizes its worth and his mission is to take what God has given us for spiritual edification and use it as a weapon of destruction. If you compromise with the devil, you will lose your anointing. A musician without an anointing is like a baseball player who strikes out every time the bases are loaded. They have the ability to hit, but they don't possess the talent to bring their fellow teammates home. Always remember, the depth of your worship determines the height of your praise.

My goal is to encourage the Christian musician, singer and praise dancer to take a non-compromising stance relative to liturgical praise and worship whether through instrumentation, voice or expression. In order to do so, we must develop a keen discernment in our approach to music because it operates both in a spiritual realm and a fallen world. To be an anointed musician

ANOINTED OFFERING OR TAINTED SACRIFICE
DECISIONS DETERMINE DESTINY

you must possess a high degree of "music integrity". When used inappropriately, music is subject to exploitation, misinterpretation, misapplication and distortion. Music can become highly manipulative in certain situations. The music minister must be careful not to allow the seed of their gift to germinate in decomposing soil. Too often, we fail to recognize that our music is not just about us. It affects every listener in either a positive, negative or neutral manner. If you are a music minister, be it in the purest form you know because God is looking at our intent, not our pretext.

As a young choir directress growing up in the church I wanted to really understand why we were instructed not to sing "worldly music". I began to search the scripture to understand the purpose and meaning of music. I have always had an appreciation for various music genres, even though my initial training and musical focus was from a gospel perspective. As I began to read the Book of Exodus, the answer to my question became very clear. I will expound upon this topic in later chapters, but today I am clear and possess no ambiguity relative to what I teach music ministers. Gospel music and liturgical praise has a distinct purpose. I have also come to appreciate that just because a song is popular or commercially promoted within the church arena does not validate it as gospel music. If it does not glorify God, edify the believer, promote positive and good intent, then it

ANOINTED OFFERING OR TAINTED SACRIFICE
DECISIONS DETERMINE DESTINY

probably is a sampling that would be better received in other venues.

God created music, so the foundation of music is and should remain in Him. When we allow our music to escape its origin, we open the door for warfare. Music can soothe and lift our spirit as well as drive our emotions. There are certain types of musical presentations that are associated with demonstrative warfare and promote messages of darkness. Heavy metal, certain forms of rap, rock, rhythm and blues and reverse production musical grooves are often scored to produce emotions that are in direct opposition to Christian values. Extremely high noise levels, the persistent repetition of motifs, a relentlessly heavy beat and aggressive body language can convey a menacing tone. Some musical experts have even taken classical music and used it to nullify its original purpose. In Carl Orff's choral work *Carmina Burana* (1935-36) and Richard Strauss's opera *Salome* (1905), music was used to heighten topics of sensuality and cruelty. So it is not just the classification or style, but the intent of the work.

In order to determine if a work of music is designed for edification, one must first identify the intention of the composition by reviewing its purpose, lyrics, the personality of the composer and review its overall expression. Every masterpiece is created with an objective.

CHAPTER I

CHAPTER ONE

THE PURPOSE

What is the purpose of our music ministry? Can I be effective in music ministry without compromising the foundational principles of Christendom established by God? How do we perfect our music departments to ensure God is getting the Glory and we are prepared for warfare? Our talents are endowments, not possessions; they are trusted to us on loan from God. We are evaluated not on the number of talents we have but on what we do with what we have. It matters not whether we have one, five or ten talents. God intends us to be fruitful with what He has entrusted into our care. We are to use them for His Glory and not merely preserve them. As we offer our service to God in faithfulness and commitment, He multiplies and expands our territory. The Bible helps to give us clear direction relative to the purpose of music; 2 Chronicles 7:6 states – *"And the priests waited on their offices: the Levites also with instruments of musick of the LORD, which David the king had made to praise the LORD, because his mercy endureth for ever, when David praised by their ministry; and the priests sounded trumpets before them, and all Israel stood."*

Anointed Offering or Tainted Sacrifice
Decisions Determine Destiny

What Does It Take to be an Effective Choir Minister/Musician?

The word *ministry* is derived from both Greek and Hebrew from a word that simply means "service." A Christian servant is someone who puts himself or herself at God's disposal for the benefit of others and for the stewardship of God's world. Therefore, I generally elect to call musicians, singers and liturgical dancers who understand their calling - music ministers. Their responsibility to the excellence of their calling is vital because they are responsible for ushering the presence of God through song. This indeed is ministry.

Music must be age appropriate. It would be awkward for a child to sing, *"I've Been Living for Jesus a Long Time";* they have not even begun to scratch the surface of life and longevity. Youth should sing appropriate songs that deliver a positive message to their contemporaries. I get excited when I see young people on fire for God. The goal of the church is not to remove the youthfulness from our youth, but rather to teach them how to truly appreciate music, how to balance their song selection and how to recognize which styles of music yield positive intent. They can dance all they want as long as they understand the boundaries, and can clearly affirm that what they are dancing to has edification and promotes wholesomeness.

Anointed Offering or Tainted Sacrifice
Decisions Determine Destiny

In the Hebrew scriptures two words are normally used for *service* and *ministry;* the first is *sharat,* which means personal service rendered to an important personage, such as a ruler or leader (Genesis 39:4), and the ministry of worship on the part of those who stand in a special relationship to God, such as priests (Exodus 28:35). The second is *abad,* which combines the meaning of "to work or to make" and "to worship." The office of a true choir minister is a blend of both terms. When agreeing to play or sing in the choir, you posture yourself as an earthen vessel willing to glorify the Lord in the image of the heavenly hosts. The heavenly hosts ceaselessly sing praise to the glory of their Creator and Lord. A choir minister acknowledges the full sacredness and importance of this godly work. We must not be careless with our calling because Jeremiah the prophet reminds us, *"Cursed is the man that doeth the work of the Lord carelessly"* (Jeremiah 48:10). Therefore we cannot be neglectful in our calling and carelessly perform the work of serving God and His people. We must be accountable and responsible. We must take self-ownership of our calling by committing our life to Christ, being conscientious, accountable, reliable, and sincere. When you take care of God's business, He will take care of you. David penned that he had never seen the righteous forsaken nor his seed begging bread. Therefore, as you present your musical gift and calling back to God in a spirit of excellence and commitment, and when He gets

ANOINTED OFFERING OR TAINTED SACRIFICE
DECISIONS DETERMINE DESTINY

the honor and Glory, you are indeed a "choir minister" whether your gift is delivered through vocal, instrumentation or dance.

When you sing, play or praise dance, do it unto the glory of the name of God. Sing not only with lips and voice, but perform with heart; dance, sing and play with mind, soul, will, desire and zeal—do it with all your being. Strive with all your strength to concentrate attentively on the words which you pronounce or the tones you play. Express your instrumentation in such a manner that they come from the depth of your soul; pronounce your words until what is in your heart reaches to another heart, and allow your expression of dance to speak the words of your emotion. The sounds of the vivifying current of your song will pour into the souls of those who hear them. When you play, play with perfection and skill. Your music should resound until the spirit within man responds in worship and humility. David ministered so intensely until it calmed the evil spirit within Saul.

May the Lord therefore give thee understanding (II Timothy 2:7) to apprehend the height of your vocation in the office of singer, musician and dancer. Bring your gift as a sacrifice to its Giver, *"for what hast thou that thou didst not receive?"* (I Corinthians. 4:7). All our talents and abilities come from an all generous God, and we have a responsibility to worship Him in

ANOINTED OFFERING OR TAINTED SACRIFICE
DECISIONS DETERMINE DESTINY

spirit and in truth. *"Come, let us worship and fall down before Christ, and let us weep before the Lord Who made us"* (Psalms 94:6).

There are certain qualities I believe make for an ideal music minister whether in the choir, an instrumentalist or praise dancer. They are key and critical to being a strong music minister. An anointed and effective music minister must be saved and filled with the Holy Ghost. They must have a love for God, His Word and His people. They must have a desire and strive to perfect their gift, and they must reflect in their style and appearance the representation of holiness. Once you have truly committed your life to Christ, the following qualities are supporting characteristics of an ideal music minster:

- **Punctuality**

    It takes a while to build up a safe, creative atmosphere, but only a second to destroy it. You should make an effort to always be in place prior to the starting time of rehearsal or service. Once rehearsal or service has begun, it is very disruptive when latecomers interrupt the flow of service. If we are doing focused warm up work, we don't want people wandering in half way through! Be timely. I know sometimes individuals may be delayed because of an unusual circumstance, but persistent latecomers are not showing respect for their fellow choir ministers or the work or the choir. They are often the ones who would benefit most from the voice training and stress-busting warm up! Stay until the service is complete and remain in position until you are dismissed. It is most disrespectful for a choir or band minister to come late and leave early.

- **Commitment**

    Commitment to the choir can be shown in many ways. It is important to be consistent week after week. To be effective, you must be willing to commit your time, talent and finances. Everyone needs to attend and show up for rehearsal, service and engagements. If for some reason you cannot attend a scheduled rehearsal, engagement or assigned service, you should communicate with your leader. Commitment and accountability are vital traits of a music ministers. You are not truly committed if you only show up for the so-called "important gigs". If you are only available for opportunities that promote your talent and gifts, then you need to check your motive meter. There is more to music ministry than just signing up. You need to become involved and be supportive of the entire program. Commitment requires a musician and trainer to prepare for rehearsal; not just show up and learn the song at the same time as the choir or soloist. Band members should set aside sufficient time to properly rehearse so their blend and balance is appropriate.

- **Responsibility**

    If you are not responsible, it is convenient to sit back and let your choir director or other members of the department do all the work. It is an easy cop-out. Yes, the Minister of Music is in charge, but the final result depends on each individual within the music department being responsible. You are responsible to learn your part and be able to retain what has been taught. Thinking your fellow choir ministers will back you up and cover you through the bits you don't know well is the sign of a lazy and thoughtless choir member as opposed to a choir minister. If every singer in the choir thought in that manner, there would be no choir!

    You have to take responsibility to be in attendance regularly (and on time), to know your part, to stay aware of rehearsal schedules, to listen to the director's instructions, and to acknowledge this is a team effort, and every team minister is responsible for the final outcome.

- **Self-awareness**

    Many people stumble through life not really paying

attention. Or if they do pay attention, it is often to the wrong thing! How many times have you been bumped in the supermarket by someone whose focus was on something else?

Often it is simply a matter of being in the moment, being present and engaged with whatever is going on at that particular point. This can be helped by focusing on the warm-up at the beginning of each session which assists in the transition between your busy daily life and the job of being in a choir.

It is by paying attention to what you are doing that helps you learn and improve. When the director points out that you are tipping your head back, check in with your own body and see what that feels like. When your fellow alto complains you're singing too loudly in his or her ear, check in with yourself and make a note of how it feels in that moment and what you can do next time.

- **Trust**
  Some people find it very uncomfortable to be in the middle of a learning process. When you first begin to learn a new song it can feel frustrating if you cannot quite nail the tune. Even when you have been singing or playing a

song for a while, you might keep tripping over some of the words.

Try not to get frustrated, but give yourself up to the process and trust that it will come out right in the end. Similarly, if the director's new structure for a song seems awkward, trust that he/she knows what they are doing and they have prepared the materials to enhance the ministry.

Throw yourself into these processes wholeheartedly and trust them. If you want to analyze or question, wait until the process is over (i.e. after the concert or at the end of term) to evaluate.

- **Attentiveness**

  Attentiveness is related to self-awareness and having a sense of the whole. For instance, an individual choir or band minister may forget where they are and start chatting with their neighbor. After all, they have finished learning their part and are, in fact, talking about important singing matters. But what they do not realize is they are missing what's going on around them.

  You need to be attentive to the director, (or you might

miss your cue), the singers around you, (you don't want to breathe at the wrong time), the overall choir sound, (make sure your part is not louder than all the others), and what your own responsibilities are (at any given moment you may be called out – so don't miss your solo!).

- **Consideration for others**

    This is all to do with respect: respect for your fellow human beings, hence respect for what you and other music ministers are doing and therefore respect for the choir as a whole. Never use your title as a hammer to destroy individuals, rather use the leadership position that has been entrusted to you as an office to build, encourage and strengthen others. Do not be a prima donna – choirs are all about teamwork. Remember what it was like when you first joined the choir – help new members. If someone in your section is struggling, do not feel superior because you have nailed it – stand next to them and gently support them.

- **Listening skills**

    You may find it surprising that singing skills are not in this list of important things for being a good choir minister. My belief is that everyone can sing and given time, everyone in the choir can reach the acceptable standard.

However, to get to that point, instead of focusing on the production of the voice, you need to pay more attention to what you are hearing. Using your self-awareness, you can begin to hear when you are getting the notes right and when you are not. Listening to others in your section will help you stay in tune, blend better and work as a unit. Reaching out to hear other sections will help you in blending the harmony, staying on pitch, enjoying and getting a better understanding of how harmony works. There may be a choir minister who desires to sing, but their ability to pitch is challenged. Therefore a choir trainer and a supportive choir minster will aide, support, and nurture their fellow minister. And finally, listening to what the director has to say can only be a good thing!

- **Skillful**

    It is critical to take time to practice and perfect your gift. No one wants a musician, singer, or praise worshiper ministering to them who has not taken time to prepare for their presentation. The Bible teaches us in II Timothy that we should study to show ourselves approved unto God, a workman that needs not to be ashamed.

    Preparation and practice helps us to become better music ministers. Everyone needs to practice; from the novice to

Anointed Offering or Tainted Sacrifice
Decisions Determine Destiny

the expert. No one is above learning. The more you know, the better you can present excellence to the King of Glory. Music precision and exactitude comes from continual rehearsal, focus, timing and experience. Always seek to enhance your knowledge and training.

- **Sense of the whole**

    It is good to get constructive feedback from your director, band minister and choir ministers, but it is a pleasure when you are able to reach out and get a sense of the music as a whole. It is great when you can hear the harmonies working, check the blend, get the volume balance of each part right, wait for the choir to take a single in-breath to start the next song, and feel part of a creative team ministering as a living organism. The Levites were charged with leading the music during worship in the Old Testament. They practiced daily to perfect their music. In addition to their priestly responsibilities, when the people settled in Canaan it was the duty of the Levites, acting as police, to guard the sanctuary. Their duties included the opening and closing of the sanctuary, the maintenance and cleaning of it and its furniture, as well as preparation of the bread of the Presence and any other required baking in connection with the sacrifices. Their responsibilities extended to assisting priests in the slaughtering and skinning of animals for sacrifice and examining lepers according to law, and looking after the Temple and its supplies, among many other tasks. (New Unger's Bible Dictionary). How many organists or lead singers do you know today who make a habit of cleaning the church restroom before they sing? As a music minister, you must understand all aspects of the ministry as well as all aspects of the music ministry.

- **Sense of humor**

    It is important to have a good sense of humor and positive attitude. A smile goes a long way in building relationships and making others feel welcome. Keep smiling even when things seem difficult. Smile during correction even if it is the umpteenth time the director has pointed out that you are getting a phrase wrong or playing the melody. Find the humor in the person standing next to you who constantly sings the wrong note – loudly! Relax, be lighthearted, and make the environment enjoyable, as the minister of music or music trainer works to correct them in love.

- **Fellowship**

    Learn how to have positive and healthy events with your fellow choir ministers outside of church. Engage in wholesome and positive group activities together that help build strong relations. You cannot have fellowship with the triune God who *is* fellowship and believe He wants you to live isolated from your sisters and brothers in Christ. When a person always keeps to themselves, something is wrong. The easiest way to invite a spirit of division is through the absence of communication. If the enemy can get us to not fellowship with one another, then he has an open door to bring unhealthy thoughts to our minds. It is much easier to minister with someone who you know has your back and cares for you, than with a complete stranger. I have seen musicians and singers who just come in time for service, play or sing and leave immediately with having no dialogue with anyone. These are called job-seekers, not music ministers. A music minister engages in communication and takes time to pray for the fellow ministers. They are concerned about the well-being of their fellow yoke-men. You do not have to be a busybody in other people's business to fellowship. A genuine greeting or short conversation will foster unity and love.

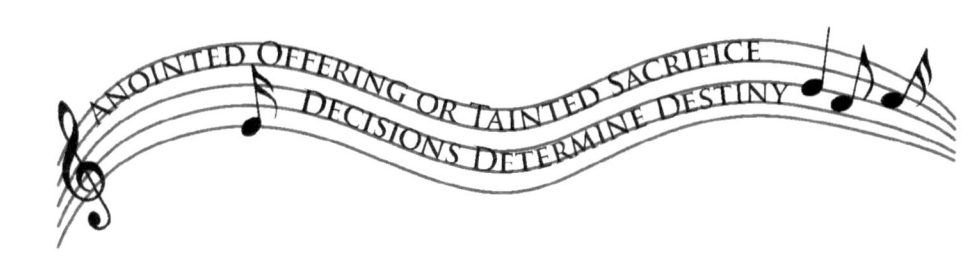

ANOINTED OFFERING OR TAINTED SACRIFICE
DECISIONS DETERMINE DESTINY

In your own words define the characteristics of an effective Music Minister.

CHAPTER II

CHAPTER TWO

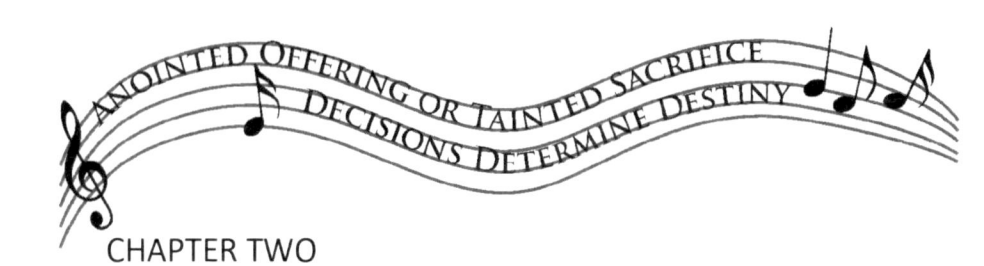

Don't Allow Your Gift to Become Clouded

Because music is a universal language and there are various interpretations and expressions, initially, it can sometimes be challenging for a music minister to decisively determine the intent of a composition. The message of the song is critical. There is music that has been birthed out of experience, while other presentations have merely been scored because of their familiarity to other sounds. I know some artists who have the same presentation of sound in each of their productions. They merely change the lyrics and a few chord progressions. But a truly gifted music minister is able to reach mankind through their anointed expression of tones and reverberations.

Your gift will make room for you, so be careful not to prostitute your talent. I know this is a bold statement, but as I have matured in my musical walk, I have repeatedly counseled musicians who have allowed their focus to be fame and money rather than purpose and destiny. Many of them have achieved varying levels of success and fortune, but most of them lack inward peace and happiness. Understand, when we alter our God-given purpose, we also alter our destiny.

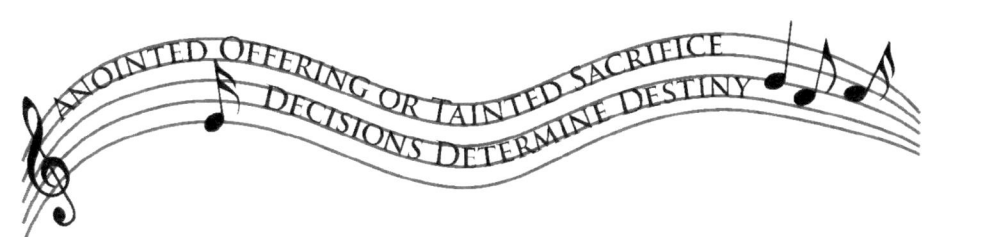

Anointed Offering or Tainted Sacrifice
Decisions Determine Destiny

Intent and discernment are such critical terms for music ministers. As musicians, we have various levels of appreciation for multiple types of musical genres. There are both blessings and lessons to be learned from them all. At one time, jazz was considered a style of music that was off limits for the church musician because of its origin. The roots of both jazz and rock can be traced back to earthly and sexual expressions. However, inherited within jazz are creative and skillful chord progressions. The myth is that because an artist has improvisatory skills and instrumental virtuosity, what they are playing is rooted in repulsive jazz.

As seasoned musicians we must be able to define whether a piece of music is an expression of jazz because of the skill and improvising of cords or if the composition has been defined by the artist as jazz because of its intent to ignite a lazy and sexual mood. A basic definition for jazz is defined as a popular music that originated among black Americans in New Orleans in the late 19th century and is characterized by syncopated rhythms and improvisation (Encarta Dictionary of North America). There are various sub-genres of jazz,(i.e. – ragtime, gospel, spiritual songs, West African rhythms and European harmonies) and all of its music was not birthed from sinful expressions, but because the

Anointed Offering or Tainted Sacrifice
Decisions Determine Destiny

overshadowing reputation of the art, even today, jazz is oftentimes associated with clubs and bars. Music ministers are reprimanded when they play distinct choir progressions associated with this type of genre because of some of the origins of its sub-genres. Closely related styles often overlap; therefore it is imperative to understand the intent and spirit of the composition. *The sin is not in the chord, but rather in how it is applied; the spirit of the artist and their objective.*

Our message is clouded when we attempt to blend what is God-purposed with the world. Music originally belonged to the church; but many artists, just like Lucifer, have defiled that which was intended for spiritual edification with reprehensible intent. Lucifer was a gifted musician but he was drawn away by his desire to be greater than his creator. Ezekiel 28 parallels the fall of the King of Tyre to that of Satan. Ezekiel 28:13-15, *"Thou hast been in Eden the garden of God; every precious stone was thy covering, the sardius, topaz, and the diamond, the beryl, the onyx, and the jasper, the sapphire, the emerald, and the carbuncle, and gold: the workmanship of thy tabrets and of thy pipes was prepared in thee in the day that thou wast created. [14]Thou art the anointed cherub that covereth; and I have set thee so: thou wast upon the holy mountain of God; thou hast walked up and down in the midst of the stones of fire. 15Thou wast perfect in thy ways from the day that thou wast created, till iniquity was found in thee."*

Like many musicians today, Lucifer took advantage of his liberties. He had within his power the ability to go back and forth from heaven to earth to spend time in God's presence, to refresh and renew, serve and then return to his rulership over the earth again. The grandeur of Lucifer's high office overwhelmed him with pride thus, he violated his right of choice when pride set in, wanting more than the earth to rule. He wanted it all, which meant taking over God's position as ruler over the entire world. His goal - defeat God and sit upon His throne in heaven.

Isaiah 14:12-15 gives us another reflection of the fall of Satan – *"How art thou fallen from heaven, O Lucifer, son of the morning! how art thou cut down to the ground, which didst weaken the nations! 13For thou hast said in thine heart, I will ascend into heaven, I will exalt my throne above the stars of God: I will sit also upon the mount of the congregation, in the sides of the north: 14I will ascend above the heights of the clouds; I will be like the most High. 15Yet thou shalt be brought down to hell, to the sides of the pit."* Be careful, because music is an influencer. When you fall, others will follow and you certainly do not want that blood on your hands. The Bible teaches that when the enemy fell he took a third of the heavenly host with him. Revelation 12:4 –*"And his tail*

ANOINTED OFFERING OR TAINTED SACRIFICE
DECISIONS DETERMINE DESTINY

drew the third part of the stars of heaven, and did cast them to the earth: and the dragon stood before the woman which was ready to be delivered, for to devour her child as soon as it was born." Be extremely careful to do the right thing when in music leadership. Remember at one time Lucifer had it all, upon losing his princely appointment; Lucifer, the once anointed cherub, is now Satan the adversary. He is a defeated being who will never have the opportunity to be restored and he does not want to see you whole.

As a musician you have influence and authority. The key is how you use it. Music ministers must never forget who the giver of our gift is and what He expects from us. We are His workmanship. If we allow ourselves to be drawn by worldly offerings of fame, fortune and pride then we are akin to Lucifer. One must recognize that the spirit of Lucifer was centered on dawning and wanting more rather than on serving. The myth states God does not have great destiny for those who are committed and stay the course. I can assure you the God of all flesh remains faithful to those who trust Him. David declared in Psalms 37:25, *"I have been young, and now am old; yet have I not seen the righteous forsaken, nor his seed begging bread"*.

CHAPTER III

CHAPTER THREE

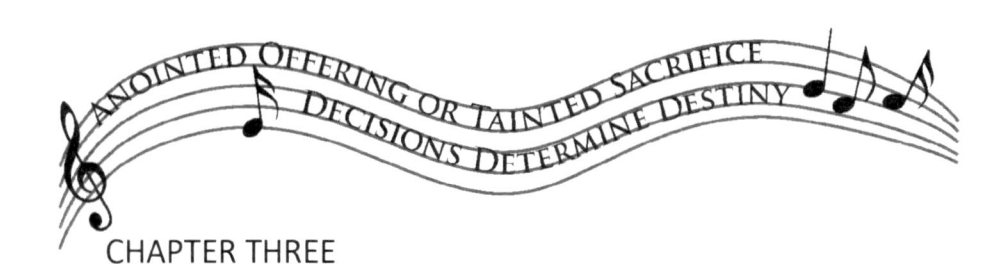

How Did We Get So Far Removed From God's Original Intent?

The answer to this question is relatively the same for any area in our lives; when we place performance or things above purpose, we lose focus. To begin to understand this question let's review from an historical perspective. The following references and resources H. M. Best, *Music Through the Eyes of Faith* (San Francisco: Harper, 1993); D. P. Hustad, *Jubilate II—Church Music in Worship and Renewal* (Carol Stream, Ill.: Hope Publishing, 1993); A. Wilson-Dickson, *The Story of Christian Music* (Batavia, Ill.: Lion, 1992) aide us in understanding certain eras of music. Edward Norman pens:

> "Martin Luther's affirmative view of music fostered one of the richest musical movements in Protestant culture. He focuses on the God given intent of music. His focus was on the Lutheran chorale, which reflects from a wide range of sacred and secular melodies and is the basis of our modern congregational hymnody. The movement arising from Luther became the framework for exciting new music by Protestant composers who

Anointed Offering or Tainted Sacrifice — Decisions Determine Destiny

dedicated their work to the church: Jan Sweelinck, Heinrich Schutz, Johann Pachelbel and Dietrich Buxtehude, to name just a few. At the height of this era one figure stands out supremely—Johann Sebastian Bach (1685-1750).

A combination of superlative skill, extraordinary energy and evident Christian commitment gives Bach's music an unusual degree of integrity and attractiveness. His nearly two hundred cantatas for the church, his moving settings of Christ's passion (from St. Matthew and St. John), the great B Minor Mass and his organ chorale preludes reveal not only a vibrant personal faith but also a thorough understanding of theology as well as consummate skill. In the society in which Bach lived, rigorous, disciplined training was a prerequisite to musical leadership, particularly in the church; good ideas were not enough.

Music really does reveal a lot, but the poetry set to it perhaps reveals even more: early Latin hymn texts stressing God's holiness and majesty; sixteenth-century texts focusing on our unworthiness, the hymns of Charles Wesley and Isaac Watts full of assurance and the prospect of eternal life. An unquestioned Trinitarian belief and a clear view of the human condition shine through the words and music of these periods

Anointed Offering or Tainted Sacrifice — Decisions Determine Destiny

leading up to the turbulent nineteenth century. It is fascinating to see what happened next.

Bach died in 1750, and Handel—also a profoundly Christian musician—died shortly thereafter. Observing what followed, we can see how the character of Christian music was unlikely to be the same again. The influence that the church had for so long exerted upon the course of music and art dropped away. The character of music changed abruptly as the focus moved from the church to the concert hall and the opera house. Music could not consider itself primarily Christian any longer, because all of its exciting new developments were taking place outside the church's sphere of influence.

We can trace how the church retreated from an increasingly hostile secular world to create its own in-house art and music: typically a sentimental, otherworldly type of expression, which has held sway in the churches up to the present day. Looking at a chorus collection of the later nineteenth century, such as Ira D. Sankey's *Sacred Songs and Solos,* we see the impact of mass production on Christian music. It became a widely disseminated, prepackaged, functional and pietistic product. Of course, there are even within these stylistic confines some attractive and effective compositions that have rightly

ANOINTED OFFERING OR TAINTED SACRIFICE
DECISIONS DETERMINE DESTINY

survived the test of time, but the overall quality of music during this period reflects a general decline in the fortunes of spiritual music."

When our focus is not Christ centered, we are likely to be drawn away by our own lust and desires. Personally, I don't take issue with the separation of music from the church to various concert halls, because I believe spiritual music can and should be played in various venues. The central issue is that of personal gain and performance for self-glorification. When our intent and purpose is driven solely by pride and selfishness, then destruction will soon follow. Pride leads to contention. The Bible teaches in Proverbs 13:10, *"Only by pride cometh contention: but with the well advised is wisdom."* So many times we fail to heed sound wisdom because we place too much value in our abilities and talents rather than the One who gifted us. We must be careful not to allow our gift to take precedence over our calling. In my opening comments, I expressed an insight that God had given to me relative to Exodus the 32nd chapter. So many artists believe that crossover music is a recent phenomena; however if you study this chapter you will see the Children of Israel experienced this during their wilderness stay.

Moses had anointed the Children of Israel prior to him going to seek the Lord. They were initially settled in their spirit. Prior to this time, their songs were praises to God for their deliverance and His

Anointed Offering or Tainted Sacrifice
Decisions Determine Destiny

provision. Because of their impatience, sin began to rule. They convinced Aaron to erect a golden calf for them to worship. While returning to the camp, Joshua told Moses he heard a war cry in the camp, but Moses knew from what the Lord had told him that the people were singing in idolatrous celebration; their song had "crossed over". Not only had their song changed, but they were involved in drunkenness and immorality. Exodus 32:17 & 18 reads, *"And when Joshua heard the noise of the people as they shouted, he said unto Moses, There is a noise of war in the camp. And he said, It is not the voice of them that shout for mastery, neither is it the voice of them that cry for being overcome: but the noise of them that sing do I hear."* If a song is written with positive and godly intent and the world embraces the song and it crosses over, God can still be glorified. That song will convey a universal message. In contrast, if a composer intentionally creates a song for the purpose of trying to have it accepted by the world, then the underpinning message is birthed because of materialism, not godly intent. God does not have to play second fiddle to anything or anyone. Ever since I studied this passage, I have been careful not to allow passion, eagerness, profligacy, avariciousness, arrogance, ignorance, impulsiveness or impetuosity to alter my song. Never allow the perceived benefits of sin to change your message or song; your blessing may be delayed, but it is not denied.

CHAPTER IV

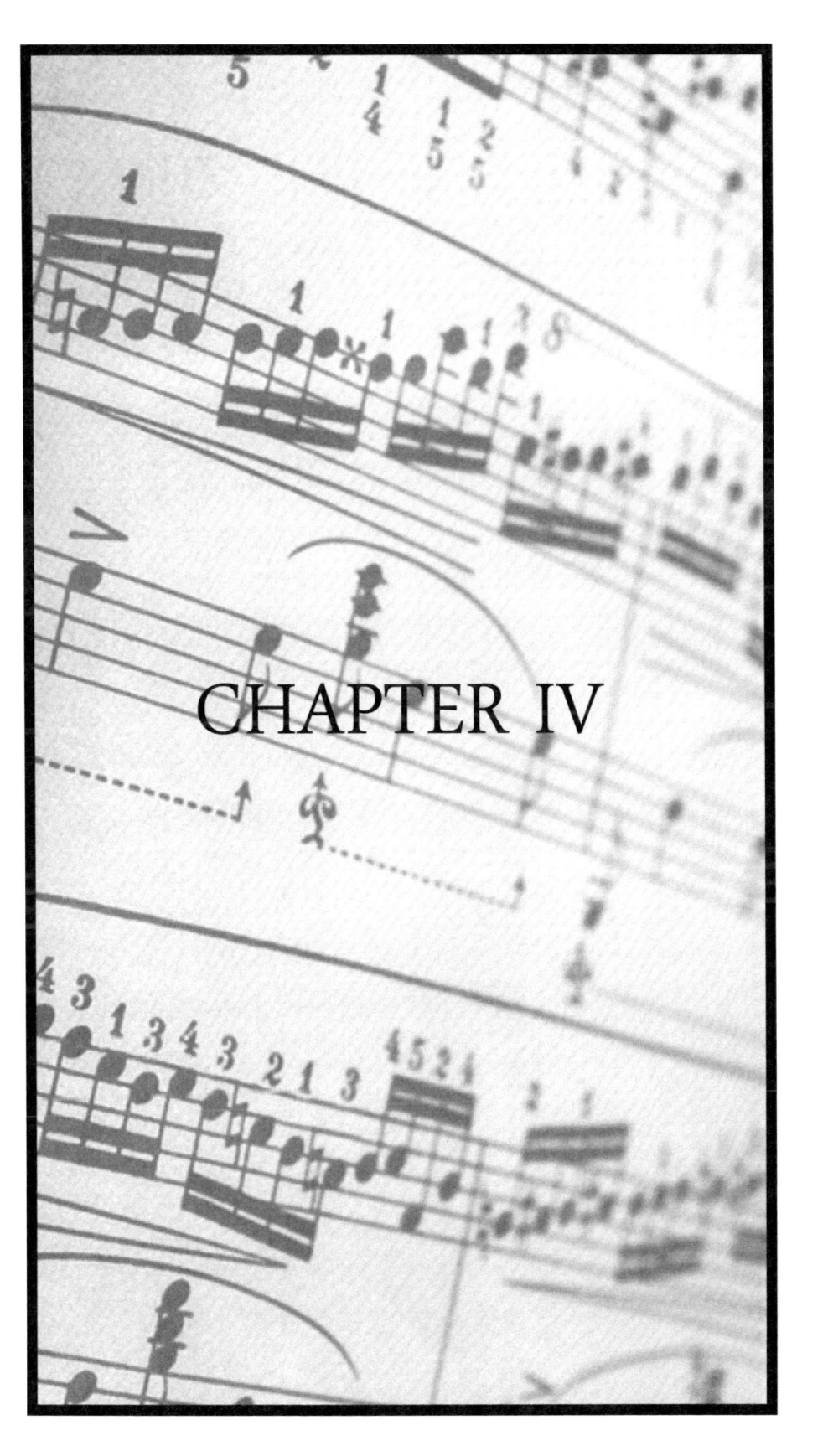

CHAPTER FOUR

How Are You Tuned?

Music carries influence and power, it produces varying emotions within. It is not just sound. Music is an expression of motions, waves and beats. Beethoven composed *Ode to Joy* at a time when he was totally deaf. He never heard the simple yet beautiful melody that some people have called the most popular song in the world. I believe music works on our subconscious; it has the ability to trigger mood and unlock deeply embedded memories. The Bible teaches that Saul had an evil spirit, but through the skillful playing of David, he was momentarily released from that spirit. In 1 Samuel 16:15-16 Saul's attendants said to him, "*See, an evil spirit from God is tormenting you. 16Let our lord command his servants here to search for someone who can play the harp. He will play when the evil spirit from God comes upon you, and you will feel better.*"

1 Samuel 16:23 - Whenever the spirit from God came upon Saul, David would take his harp and play. Relief would come to Saul, he would feel better, and the evil spirit would leave him. *When the music minister is anointed, skillfully prepared and uses appropriate chord progressions, they too can be equipped with the ability to discharge evil spirits.*

Anointed Offering or Tainted Sacrifice
Decisions Determine Destiny

While reading on the topic of cognitive neuroscience of music in the Wikipedia Encyclopedia, I was intrigued with its content, which stated emotions induced by music activate frontal brain regions compared to emotions elicited by other stimuli.

> "Music is able to create an incredibly pleasurable experience that can be described as "chills". Blood and Zatorre (2001) used PET to measure changes in cerebral blood flow while participants listened to music that they knew to give them the "chills" or any sort of intensely pleasant emotional response. They found that as these chills increase, many changes in cerebral blood flow are seen in brain regions such as the amygdale, orbitofrontal cortex, ventral striatum, midbrain, and the ventral medial prefrontal cortex. Many of these areas appear to be linked to reward and motivation, emotion and arousal and are also activated in other pleasurable situations. Nucleus accumbens (a part of striatum) is involved in both music related emotions, as well as rhythmic timing.
>
> When unpleasant melodies are played, the posterior cingulate cortex activates, which indicates a sense of conflict or emotional pain. The right hemisphere has also been found to be correlated with emotion, which can also activate areas in the cingulate in times of emotional pain,

Anointed Offering or Tainted Sacrifice — Decisions Determine Destiny

specifically social rejection (Eisenberger). This evidence, along with observations, has led many musical theorists, philosophers and neuroscientists to link emotion with tonality. This seems almost obvious because the tones in music *seem* like a characterization of the tones in human speech, which indicate emotional content. The vowels in the phonemes of a song are elongated for a dramatic effect, and it seems as though musical tones are simply exaggerations of the normal verbal tonality."

We are indeed wonderful and uniquely created. If we integrate the learning of cognitive neuroscience with the spiritual aspect of mind, body and soul, we can clearly understand how the anointed music of David affected the emotions of Saul.

A music minster must be attuned and understand that sound progressions of properly pitched root chords will have a calming effect on individuals; just as diminished or augmented chords when played off pitch will enrage certain emotions. As music ministers, we must shield our heart, mind and soul because once we ignite certain emotions, there will be an actionable response. We must be keenly aware of what our music appetite craves, because listening to music is a psychosomatic encounter.

Many years ago I read a research study in Altern Ther Health Medicine 1998 Jan;4(1):75-84 (McCraty) related to the psychology of

Anointed Offering or Tainted Sacrifice
Decisions Determine Destiny

music and its effects. This study investigated the impact of different types of music on tension, mood, and mental clarity. The researchers took 144 subjects and completed a psychological profile before and after listening for 15 minutes to four types of music (grunge rock, classical, New Age, and designer). With grunge rock music, significant increases were found in hostility, sadness, tension, and fatigue, and significant reductions were observed in caring, relaxation, mental clarity, and vigor. In contrast, after listening to the designer music (music designed to have specific effects on the listener), significant increases in caring, relaxation, mental clarity, and vigor were measured; significant decreases were found in hostility, fatigue, sadness, and tension. The results for New Age and classical music were mixed. Feeling shifts among subjects were observed with all types of music. Designer music was most effective in increasing positive feelings and decreasing negative feelings. Results suggest that designer music may be useful in the treatment of tension, mental distraction, and negative moods.

According to Laurence O'Donnell, III, "The effects of music can be seen in various greats such as Thomas Jefferson Music helped Thomas Jefferson write the Declaration of Independence. When he could not figure out the right wording for a certain part, he would play his violin to help him get the words from his brain onto the paper. Albert Einstein is recognized as one of the smartest men who ever lived. A little-known fact about Einstein is that when he was young he did extremely poor in school. His grade school teachers told his parents to take him out of school because he was "too stupid to learn" and it would be a waste of resources for the school to invest time and energy in his education. The school suggested that his parents get Albert an easy, manual labor job as soon as they could. His mother did not think that Albert was "stupid". Instead of following the school's advice, Albert's parents bought him a violin. Albert became good at the violin. Music was the key that helped Albert Einstein become one of the smartest men who has ever lived. Einstein himself says that the reason he was so smart is because he played the violin. He loved the music of Mozart and Bach the most. A friend of Einstein, G.J. Withrow, said that the way Einstein figured out his problems and equations was by improvising on the violin."

The top engineers from Silicon Valley are all musicians. Napoleon understood the enormous power of music. He summed it up by saying, "Give me control over he who shapes the music of a nation, and I care not who makes the laws".

"Tests on the effects of music on living organisms besides humans have shown that special pieces of music (including The Blue Danube) aid hens in laying more eggs. Music can also help cows to yield more milk. Researchers from Canada and the former Soviet Union found that wheat will grow faster when exposed to special ultrasonic and musical sounds. Rats were tested by psychologists to see how they

Anointed Offering or Tainted Sacrifice
Decisions Determine Destiny

would react to Bach's music and rock music. The rats were placed into two different boxes. Rock music was played in one of the boxes while Bach's music was played in the other box. The rats could choose to switch boxes through a tunnel that connected both boxes. Almost all of the rats chose to go into the box with the Bach music even after the type of music was switched from one box to the other."

Music reaches the heart of the listener and causes the emotions within that individual to respond. Concert pitch is set at A=432hz, the exactness of this pitch can have profound positive effects on consciousness and also on the cellular level of our bodies. Whenever the pitch is adjusted it can be both heard and felt. An article released by Brian T. Collins suggests that even the slightest modification to an A=440 Hz pitch generates an unhealthy effect or anti-social behavior in the consciousness of human beings. A=440 Hz as a standard for concert pitch possibly may bring an unnatural 8 Hz dissonant change in how we think. Our inner ear for example works on the basis of Phi dampening. The waters of our inner ears rely on Fibonacci spiral dampening through the seashell like structure of the cochlea to keep us *feeling* centered or grounded. This Fibonacci spiral shape helps

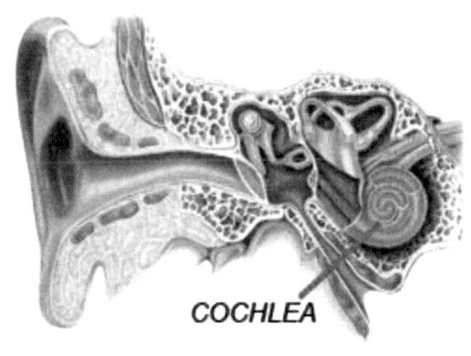

COCHLEA

Anointed Offering or Tainted Sacrifice — Decisions Determine Destiny

cancel out certain inertial standing wave interference patterns, like a Helmholtz resonator, in order to keep us properly balanced with the natural environment around us. When the inner ear is in stress by artificial means, we can experience a type of "fog like" condition or feel "spaced out".

Maria Renold's book, *Intervals Scales Tones and the Concert Pitch C=128 Hz*, claims conclusive evidence that 440 Hz and raising concert pitch above scientific "C" Prime=128 Hz (Concert A=432 Hz) disassociates the connection of consciousness to the body and creates anti-social conditions in humanity.

Some audiophiles have also reported that A=432 Hz music seems to be non-local and can appear to fill a room, whereas A=440 Hz can be perceived as directional or linear in sound propagation. The A=432 is a root of triad root of the Prime=128 Hz. Raising concert pitch may cause stress or warping of acoustic instruments and may seriously damage a singer's vocal chords according to some professional opera singers.

If we examine the 20th century collective consciousness and the use of A=440 Hz as possible pitch control in mass media pushed through radio & television as the "British Invasion" of Rock & Roll, we see the potential anti-social behaviors and possible dangers of using higher and higher pitches as central references for music. High pitch excretes emotions.

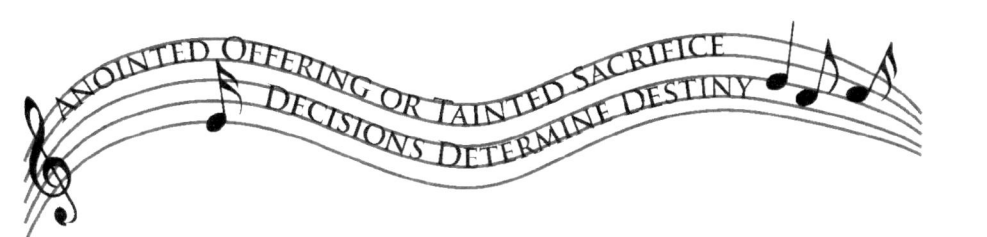

Anointed Offering or Tainted Sacrifice
Decisions Determine Destiny

This information was well-known over one hundred years ago and Rudolf Steiner warned mankind that using "*luciferic brightness*" and "*arhimanic*" tones in music could bring a condensing of greed forces in the west instead of "C" Prime=128 Hz (Concert A=432 Hz) which he mentioned was "*Christ*" consciousness of ascendant energy and angel "*Michael*" sun tone energy in the collective awareness in the evolution of man. The number three represents the trinity nature of the Godhead.

Why is perfect pitch so critical for a professional music minister? I was taught as a young musician that pitch was important because our body, bone and spin were tuned to "C" and all of the elements that influenced earth and sky worked in harmony to the "C" principle, and when we are misaligned, everything is off. Recently, I reviewed an article written by Kathleen Goss PhD, Assistant Professor in the Department of Surgery Research at the University of Chicago on Dr. June Leslie Wieder and her book, *The Song of the Spine*, which reveals many of her findings relative to this matter. Dr. Wieder, a chiropractor, has developed a healing technique called bone toning, which uses pure musical tones to bring the spinal vertebrae, as well as the subtler energy systems of the body, into attunement and alignment.

Similarly, Dr. Wieder reveals that spinal vertebrae are individually tuned to the notes of the diatonic scale in C, including the "black

ANOINTED OFFERING OR TAINTED SACRIFICE — DECISIONS DETERMINE DESTINY

keys" of the piano for the reverse curves of the cervical and lumbar segments of the spine. Her studies reveal that each bone of the spine has its own tone and frequency, and applying specific vibrational frequencies directly to the vertebrae generates a sympathetic response that activates the embedded harmonics that help maintain healthy functioning.

Dr. Goss's article continues to explain "the spine is shaped like the curvature of a wave. The song of the spine is the Pythagorean music of the spheres. Dr. Wieder lays out a rich and complex history of healing traditions and innovations utilizing sound, music, light, electricity, and other vibratory modalities. She describes manipulative therapies that aim to restore balance in the skeleton, muscles, nerves, cells, mind, and spirit, through properly applied frequencies of energy or touch. She shows how sound manifests as form, as revealed in the science of Cymatics, and how we can access the unconscious wisdom of the organism through muscle testing, or applied kinesiology."

So the music minster must have clarity of sound and be properly tuned spiritually to effectively minister in song. The slightest shift can cause disruption and imbalance. When a musician is attuned to worship, their song and presentation is not about them, but focused on Him. In Him we live, move and have our being – this should be our musical testimony.

CHAPTER V

CHAPTER FIVE

HIS GLORY IS YOUR DISTINGUISING FACTOR

Often asked are the questions, *How can I experience the Glory of the Lord?* and *How can I experience the great honor, a state of absolute happiness, gratification, and contentment the God?* Many times in our walk with the Lord, we ask the Lord to reveal Himself or His Will to us. We sincerely want to experience the Power and the Glory of the Lord. But what are we really asking God, when we say we want to know Him in the power of His resurrection? His resurrection was so painful and costly that it could only bring Glory to God.

If we sincerely want to experience the Power and the Glory of the Lord we must examine what is involved in the "ask". What we are really saying to God, is *I want to know you in the power of your resurrection.* His resurrection was so painful and costly until it could only bring Glory to God. Even though Christ worked many miracles, it was the power in His death and resurrection that ultimately distinguished Him as the Son of God.

Moses posed the same question to the Lord and asked God to see His Glory. The Lord instructed Moses to lead the Children of Israel to the Promised Land - Canaan; a land flowing with milk and

Anointed Offering or Tainted Sacrifice
Decisions Determine Destiny

honey. There was just one major problem, the Lord told Moses I want you to lead the people but, "I will not be going with you." Moses wanted to know, well God if you are not going with me, then who will you send with me, remember now God; these are your people. God answered by assuring Moses that His presence would accompany him. So now the question comes to mind, *What is the difference between God's presence and His Glory?* God's presence is the knowledge that assures one of His existences. It is His abiding force that introduces His Glory, and everything else we need, will be supplied. His presence ushers in His Glory. God reveals Himself in many ways. He does not always have to be physically present for us to experience His presence. Paul declared in Philippians 2:12 *"Wherefore my beloved as ye have always obeyed, not as in my presence only, but now much more in my absence, work out your own salvation with fear and trembling."* David penned in Psalms 16:11 – *"In thy presence is the fullness of Joy."* So you can have completeness just by His presence, but Moses wanted to experience more than just His presence. He wanted to know His divine Glory. His divine Glory is the total essence of who God is; it is the assurance that He has taken complete residence and total possession. Moses needed an assurance as well as a point of differential to know God was leading and directing him, so he asked the Lord to "show him His Glory". For the believer who walks in the Favor of God, His

ANOINTED OFFERING OR TAINTED SACRIFICE
DECISIONS DETERMINE DESTINY

presence is the assurance of Mathew 8:20 – *"For where two or three are gathered together in my name, there am I in the midst of them."* Mathew 28:20, *"lo, I am with you always, even unto the end of the world"*. He declares He will not leave us nor forsake us. He assures us His presence will give us rest. It gives us courage in life's battles and helps us to comfort the trials of this life. As music ministers we are not exempt from fiery trials or temptations.

In actuality the testing of music ministers is sometimes more intense because the enemy also recognizes if one is highly anointed they will be effective Kingdom builders and it will be more difficult to displace them. When we are strong in our faith, we cannot be easily altered. Knowing the presence of God is with us helps us to stay the course. I am convinced some of the greatest attacks presented in my life are because of what I teach and how I live. I do not believe it is necessary for a music minister to compromise their gift and calling in order to be blessed. We should not convolute messages with that of the world. God is not begging for attention, He simply provides opportunity for the music minister to "do the right thing" concerning Him. If we fail to worship and adore Him, it is our loss, not His. He will get the glory even if a rock has to cry out; I am determined not to let the rock cry for me.

Anointed Offering or Tainted Sacrifice
Decisions Determine Destiny

Isaiah declares in 43:2, *"When thou passest through the water, I will be with thee; and through the rivers, they shall not overflow thee: when thou walkest through the fire, thou shalt not be burned; neither shall the flame kindle upon thee."* His presence is something He has granted to those who walk upright before Him. When you walk through the valley of the shadow of death, you don't have to fear for He is with you. Man in our current state cannot handle the full Glory of God; so God gave Moses a glimpse of His goodness. His goodness is His Glory and it is granted to the music worshiper who continually stays in His presence. David declared in Psalms 63:2 – *"if I see your Glory I have seen you."* Peter teaches that the spirit of His Glory rests upon us. When Peter and the disciples were asleep upon the mount, after they awoke, they saw Christ's Glory, and the two men who were standing with Him. An effective music minister will not only experience the blessing of the Lord now, but what we have today is just a mere sample of what is to come; we shall see Him as He is, in His full Glory. A reward for our faithfulness and diligence will be granted to every music worshiper who stays the course. Experiencing the Glory of God does not only involve possessing His presence, but being the reflection of His likeness. When you have truly dedicated your gift to the Glory of God, He indeed distinguishes you. When you are a true music minister, your goal is to produce a quality sound that has the ability to transcend all

Anointed Offering or Tainted Sacrifice — Decisions Determine Destiny

cultures. Its intent should not be solely designed to appease the world, but rather to minister to them. When your composition reaches the heart of man, it will cause others who are not in the body to be affected by it. That effect may sometimes introduce your composition to a crossover market; an arena that it was not originally intended for, but your focus should and must be ministry. *Oh Happy Day*, *You Brought the Sunshine*, and *Never Could Have Made It* were all written to minister to the Body of Christ. However, because of their effectiveness, they are recognized and appreciated as global works of art.

It is an honor to be distinguished by your peers, but the greatest recognition an artist achieves is to have God Himself pleased with your ministry, your lifestyle, your intent and your effectiveness. In doing so, you will join coronation spiritually anointed chief musicians, singer and worshipers in glory. The real essence of *power* is the ability to make the right choice based on the *truth* of the Word.

CHAPTER VI

CHAPTER SIX

THE AUTHENTIC SOUND OF GOSPEL MUSIC

Is there a process that develops a gifted individual into a true music minister? Does the Church genuinely have a unique and distinctive sound?

Many people have tried to strip the dignity and authenticity from gospel music by coupling and commingling it with unnecessary hard beats and riffs which can alter the pureness from the gospel sound. Gospel music is music that has you "spellbound or awesome-struck" by God because it spiritually engulfs your being. I want to be clear, there is nothing wrong with certain riffs and scales that accompany a composition, but when a musician or singer is only able to produce a series of repeated tones with no bottom and beats with varying beats and no purpose, it is a sign of lack of training and immaturity. Understanding your craft, its history and what has made others within that category successful is critical for a music minister. Don't be distracted. God has fixed your charter to handle success.

Before I created my company, I studied and prepared myself for the journey. I did not wait until it was "show time" to prepare myself, but with diligence and assiduousness, I equipped myself

ANOINTED OFFERING OR TAINTED SACRIFICE
DECISIONS DETERMINE DESTINY

for a business career. So is it for musicians, singers and worshipers. You must be willing to commit the necessary time to develop and continually enhance your gift. It is not enough to learn a few cords or sections and think you have arrived. As a student of Christian Music and its musical art form, you must be willing to commit to becoming a gospel music expert. Within this category, there is a vast array of learning from the novice to the professional - everyone must practice daily in order to continue to perfect their skill. Additionally, it is important to have a good understanding of the business aspect of music. It is a "musical sin" for a musician, singer or worshiper to be gifted and not desire to enhance their gift; I might be crossing the line, but I surely do feel that way. A lazy musician, singer or worshiper has little value to the Kingdom. I think I am safe in asserting that, lack of education and training is a hindrance, weight and impediment to the advancement of music ministry. If you are serious about music ministry, it is critical that you invest in the development of your gift and acquire the tools necessary to perfect your calling. Always remain a student of the art.

Gospel music has more history than any other genre, because it all began with this art form. The church truly does has an authentic sound and when ministered properly, even the untrained ear can distinguish it. The hymns of the church are distinct and should be played and sung in a way that lifts your

Anointed Offering or Tainted Sacrifice *Decisions Determine Destiny*

spirit and resounds a message. The study of hymnody and hymnology is cosmic. The *Catholic Encyclopedia* has extensive research relative to these topics. It defines hymnody as a term taken from the Greek (*hymnodia*), which means exactly "hymn song", but as the hymn-singer as well as the hymn-poet are included under (*hymnodos*), so they also include under hymnody the hymnal verse or religious lyric. Hymnology is the science of hymnody or the historico-philogical investigation and an esthetic estimation of hymns and hymn writers. I could devote multiple pages to the history and historical writers of hymns and still not give proper credence to its worth. There are liturgical hymnodies which were designed for the priest, there are missal or the gradual hymnodies, Non-liturgical hymnodies which generally fall within the categories of (1) Canticles (cantiones). These are spiritual songs which do not belong to the liturgy, but still were employed after and during the liturgy, without being incorporated, like the tropes, with it. They gave rise to the folk-songs, from which the canticles are differentiated by being written in ecclesiastical Latin and being sung by the official cantors, but not by the people; and (2) Motets (*muteti, motelli*). These are the artistic forerunners of the canticles and nearly related to the tropes of the worship, inasmuch as they grew out of the Gradual responses of the worship. In general, they may be defined as polyphonic church songs which were to be sung *a cappella* (without musical accompaniment).

To be a music minster without having an appreciation for hymns is similar to trying to drive an automobile without an engine. Yet so many singers and musicians are unprepared in this area. As I look at the landscape of up and coming artists, too many of them cannot sing or play some of the most traditional and straightforward hymns. My challenge to each and every music minister is to commit to learning a different hymn each week; in doing so, you dramatically enlarge your scope of songs, improve your aptitude and noticeably enrich your presentation. We should challenge our young musicians to properly practice hymns on a daily basis; they should learn how to play them in the key signature scored, as well as in every key. They should be expected to have a portfolio of hymns they have perfected. Too often underdeveloped music ministers are encouraged to learn the latest tunes and songs. In doing so, we handicap their ability and place a governor on their capacity to exceed beyond the norm.

Not only does the church have an originating resonance, but each worshiping experience has uniqueness to it. Within the Christian church there also is a multiplicity of denominations that required trained and anointed vessels to usher in worship. A music minister must be prepared to present their gift in various

Anointed Offering or Tainted Sacrifice — Decisions Determine Destiny

types of settings. They must also be able to effectively adapt in any environment; whether performing for a Catholic Mass, Episcopal Ordination Service, a music festival, a European venue, a corporate sponsored event, a media production or recording, or during a lively Pentecostal worship experience. Having the appropriate selection properly prepared is critical. You must know and understand who your audience is. The level of anointing within you will operate in any setting, but the delivery and texture of your presentation should align with the event. Imagine someone singing the latest contemporary hip-hop gospel tune at an event sponsored by the local Department of Aging. Within ten minutes everyone in the audience would be looking for their walkers or searching for the *off* position on their hearing aids. It is just as absurd to sing, *"I'm Alive, I'm Alive"* at a funeral.

I recently attended a wedding in which the groom was marrying for the third time. The singer at the wedding sang a song with the lyrics, *"You are my true love, you and only you have my heart."* I began to ponder on those words and thought, "I wonder – if this is his *true* love, I am sure the other two women must have been recipients of his *false* love, and I don't even want to imagine what he gave them in place of his heart." You must know and understand your audience as well as the environment.

Anointed Offering or Tainted Sacrifice
Decisions Determine Destiny

Gospel music is ever-evolving. At one time all songs were considered contemporary. But understanding the history of music and having an appreciation and understanding of the various eras in which gospel music was crafted, will broaden your capacity as a music minister. As you perfect your gift and talent, studying the musical skill set of historical gospels legends such as Thomas Dorsey, Sallie and Roberta Martin, James Cleveland, Mattie Moss-Clark, Thomas Whitfield, Charles Nicks, Mahalia Jackson, Benny Cummings, Walter Hawkins, J.C. White, B.C. and M., Isaac Douglas, Jessy Dixon, James Lenox, Donald Vails, Bill Moss, Willie Mae Ford-Smith, Timothy Wright, James Moore, Maceo Woods, Rance Allen, Clara Ward, Albertina Walker, Danniebelle Hall, Clay Evans, Lucious Hall, Charles Hayes, Shirley Caesar, Inez Andrews, Dorothy Norwood, Bobbie Jones, Richard Smallwood, James Cambers, Marvin Winans, Myrna Summers, Douglas Miller, Rosie Haynes, Father Hayes, André Crouch, Beverly, , The Hawkins Family, The Barrett Sisters, The O'Neal Twins, The Blind Boys of Alabama, The Mighty Clouds of Joy, The Consolers. The William Brothers, The Clark Sisters, The Winans Family, The Davis Sisters, The Pace Family, Chicago Mass Choir, Wisconsin Community Choir, Mississippi Mass Choir, Institutional, DSW Choir, LA Mass, Thompson Community Singers, S.E. Michigan State Choir, S.E. Texas Mass Choir, Cosmopolitan Church Choir, Star of Bethlehem, and countless others afford you the

ANOINTED OFFERING OR TAINTED SACRIFICE
DECISIONS DETERMINE DESTINY

opportunity to experience a broad array of gospel styles. Examining the art forms of these and other gifted musical giants will give you an expanded platform to perfect your ability and musical expression. Gospel music is appreciated and sung throughout the world and generally when you hear it, you know it. It is distinctly rich in base and tone. The over arching sound is clean and it carries a melody of praise.

CHAPTER VII

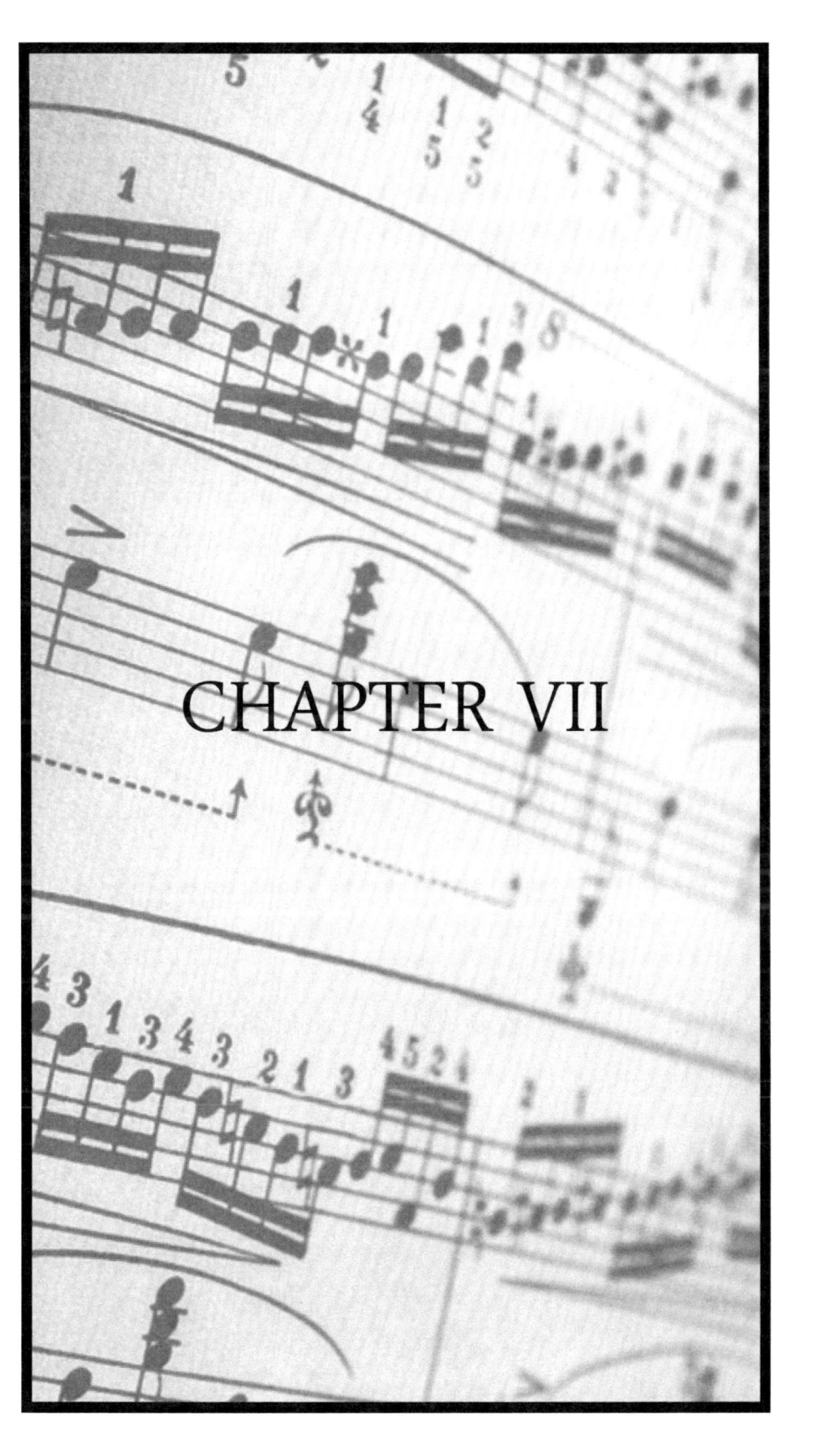

CHAPTER SEVEN

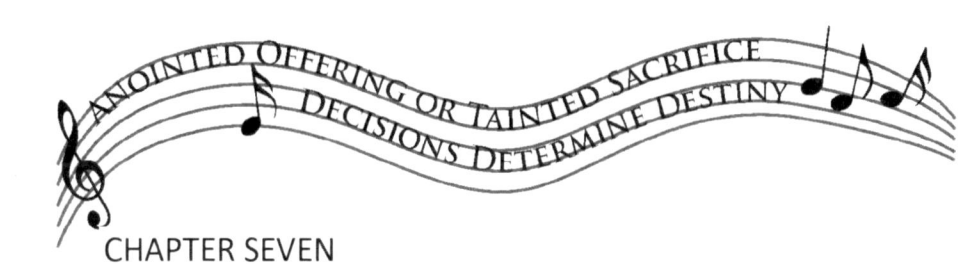

THE LIFE OF THE ARTIST

This has become such an important topic. The reflection of the exterior of a person is a direct correlation to their inner person. As in every career a person must prepare and plan for success and so must a music minister. Excellence has a definite look and our responsibility is to present excellence in our calling. So many musician and singers believe they can live how they please and do whatever they want and God will still use them because they are gifted. Well, God used a donkey, but that does not mean He desires to have a donkey sit at the table with Him. We want to present ourselves in such a way that we are invited to commune with Christ and be His representative. In order to be an effective music minister, you must be saved, and you have to fast and pray to stay grounded. Take time to meditate on Him and read His Word. Once the Word becomes a living epistle in you, your appetite for sin dissipates. You no longer look at how close to the line you can get before you sin, but rather how close to God you can get to experience His anointing.

No musician, singer or dancer is so talented that God has to use them. Music is an art form and it has a tendency to draw individuals who are more artistic. You are artistic, not crazy. Just

Anointed Offering or Tainted Sacrifice
Decisions Determine Destiny

because one is inventive or creative does not mean they should lower their standards. If you desire a sinful lifestyle, then you should perform in the club and leave the ministering to true music ministers. Just because one is gifted, does not give them special privileges when it comes to Christian lifestyle. The musician needs to be holy, the singer needs to be holy; we all need to be holy. Without holiness, no man shall see the Lord.

I often ask musicians if they would want an individual to serve them if they knew the individual had just come from the bathroom and not washed their hands. They all answer – *NO!* If that indeed is the case, explain to me why certain musicians and singers believe they can club and perform all types of sinful acts and then come into the sanctuary to take a leading part in worship. Why would they play God like that? It is because they are lifted up in pride and do not understand that their anointing is sacred. This type of behavior is called "foul praise" and whether you realize it or not, it is a simulation of truth. When a musician lives in this compromising state, their music becomes a timbering sound and has an undertone of obscurity to it. I have been told by musicians that they accept compromising gigs because they need the money. Wow, we all could use a little extra money. What they are really saying is "money" is the driving force, not their dependency on Christ, the great sustainer and provider. If how you gain your substance is derived from sinful activity, you should carefully examine your stance with Christ; because in your haste, you did not remember that He will not dwell in an unclean temple.

Lifestyle is also important because generally music ministers are on stage each time they minister. Everyone from the child to the faithful back seat attendee is watching. The enemy loves to give others justification as to why they do not have to live holy by using artists with questionable lifestyles as examples. Whether you are saved or not, smoking is not good. Singers need all the space in their lungs, and when you smoke you violate your health. A music minister's lifestyle requirements are that of every other believer. Look the part, act the part and be the part of the body that reflects the image of Christ. When you are set for ministry, the focus should not be on you. You should dress modest and your appearance should be fresh. Always wear robes or appropriate fitting garments when ministering.

The following statements are excerpts from a training manual I wrote and share with the choir ministers who serve with me at our local ministry:

> The type of music performed at Holy Redeemer Church of God In Christ should always be Christian, Reviewed Classical, Gospel, Reviewed Contemporary and Worship

Anointed Offering or Tainted Sacrifice
Decisions Determine Destiny

compositions or music for the arts. We are not a ministry that embraces secular music in worship, therefore all musicians and music leaders must adhere to this principle. A prelude should introduce and set the pace for the service. It should be started approximately ten minutes before the service and consist of lively music that is of the same nature as that of the sermon. If it is an evangelistic sermon, the music should be evangelistic as well. The music for every service whether it be a wedding, funeral, worship, special or social Event, concert or graduation should align the purpose of the service.

The choir and praise team should set the pace for the service. The choir loft is one of the first areas a person notices when they are seated for service. Musicians and choir should always be in uniform and be prepared to minister. Your ministry begins before you enter the sanctuary. The choir is on stage and up front for everyone to see; therefore anything that takes away from the unity of the spirit should not be worn or visible to the congregants. Current styles or trends may be appropriate for individual preference, but when we enter into worship, we must adorn ourselves for worship. The Levites robed themselves in preparation for worship. The choir ministers

Anointed Offering or Tainted Sacrifice
Decisions Determine Destiny

and musicians should not be texting and inattentive during the service. Choir ministers should not enter and leave the choir loft at will. There should be established protocol for the entrance and departure if necessary. If a choir minister is late, they should sit in the audience and not disrupt the setting of the choir unless approved by the music leader. The choir should be prepared for the service, having practiced all of the songs to be sung and have a knowledge of the hymn numbers so they will not have to whisper them around or pass an open songbook down the rows, either of which would be a distraction.

In order for musicians and singers to be effective, there must be unity. The Holy Redeemer Department of Music will strive to have a harmonious relationship with each music minster on a continual basis. Our foundational scriptures are: II Chronicles 5:13, 14 " ... *the trumpeters and singers were as one, to make one sound to be heard in praising and thanking the Lord; and when they lifted up their voice (singular) ... then the house of the Lord was filled with a cloud ... so that the priests could not stand to minister by reason of the cloud; for the glory of the Lord had filled the house of God.*"

Anointed Offering or Tainted Sacrifice
Decisions Determine Destiny

Acts 2:1-4 *"And when the day of Pentecost was fully come, they were all with one accord in one place, and suddenly there came a sound from heaven as of a rushing mighty wind, and it filled all the house where they were sitting. And there appeared unto them cloven tongues ... and they were all filled with the Holy Ghost, and began to speak with other tongues... "*

The music ministry of a church should be virtually transparent, like the fish tank of an aquarium. No one should really notice it, but if it wasn't there what a mess there would be. Your purpose for ministering is not to bring attention or glory to you, but to Him. Music adds to the beauty of the service and positions the hearts of people to receive the Word. It leads the believer into the worship of God and softens the heart of the non-believer. We are responsible for ushering in the presence of God so His people will receive the Word with a glad heart and open mind. We are vessels used by God for His Will and His Purpose; therefore we must live a life that is pleasing to Him.

When the Levites and patriarchs of old offered sacrifices to God, they did so within specific guidelines. A clear distinction also was made between clean and unclean animals. Offering sacrifices to idols was prohibited as well as sacrificing blemished animals.

Anointed Offering or Tainted Sacrifice
Decisions Determine Destiny

The sacrifice had to be offered to God first. He did not and will never accept carve outs. Sacrifices not in accordance to the law were rejected and considered idolatrous. Paul exhorts believers to present their whole lives as "living sacrifices" to God. In terms of worship that was acceptable to Yahweh, sacrifices presented with pure motive were essential for maintaining a positive relationship with Him. If God is asking for our whole body, why would we think He would accept a portion of what He has required? As a music minister, you have to make a choice. Is it all God, or my will and my way?

CONCLUSION

Conclusion

We have been blessed with musical gifts and callings and we have a responsibility to ensure the intent of our music is God focused. As anointed musical leaders with sanctity we promote compositions that uplift and enhance mankind. As we forge forward to new horizons and our place of destiny, we must be cognate that our composition and presentation is a reflection of intent of our heart and the ministry of Christ. With anointing and positive intent our music and worship must glorify God, edify the believer and promote wholesomeness. We must not abort our mission by compromising our talents or yielding to self-emotions; our stance for anointed music must be clearly communicated by action, word and deed. As effective worshipers, we have a responsibility to promote music excellence. The lyrics in our compositions should reflect a message of hope and deliverance. We should never give opportunity for the enemy to have any influence in our song. As we perfect our sound to reflect His glory we must continue to challenge ourselves relative to music purpose and intent. We want to challenge young musicians to learn the foundational genres of gospel music and encourage them to love and appreciate the three "H's" - History, Hymns and Humility.

Is your anointing so powerful until the Priest cannot minister?

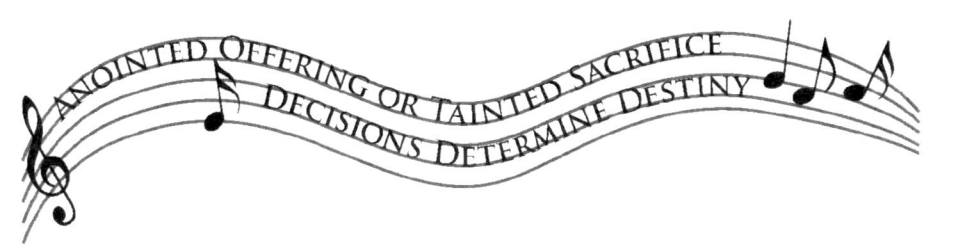

ANOINTED OFFERING OR TAINTED SACRIFICE
DECISIONS DETERMINE DESTINY

The following are questions to assist you in determining if you are operating within the fullness of your calling:

- *Are you saved?*
- *Are you filled with the Holy Ghost?*
- *Are you both committed and faithful?*
- *Are you anointed?*
- *Is your gift for the Glory of God, edification of the believer and the unification of mankind to Christ?*
- *Do you operate with excellence in your calling?*
- *Do you take time to measure the effectiveness of your gift?*
- *Are you willing to receive instruction and advice?*
- *Do you know why you were chosen?*
- *Do you challenge yourself daily to improve?*
- *Have others grown in Christ because of your gift?*
- *Is your ministry effective?*
- *Do you look like a representative of Holiness?*
- *Do you see the purpose for your calling?*
- *Have you taken a non-comprising stance?*

Only you can truthfully answer these questions. I can assure you if you can respond with an affirmative *yes*, you are indeed a music minister.

In contrast if you answer with an affirmative *yes* to the following questions, you should consider a reevaluation of your purpose:

- ❖ Is your gift personally focused?
- ❖ Will you exercise your gift in any venue regardless of the environment?
- ❖ Does the financial benefit determine if you will operate in your gift?
- ❖ Is your gift the center of attraction?
- ❖ Is your gift the reason why you exist?
- ❖ Do you elect to exercise your gift at will?
- ❖ Will you perform your gift even if the intent of the gig is to promote ungodliness?
- ❖ Do you care that individuals may experience moods of depression and anxiety because of your gift?
- ❖ Do you seek to be appreciated because of your gift?
- ❖ Is the reason people accept you dependent on your gift?

I challenge every music minister to assess their godly purpose as they ascend to new horizons.

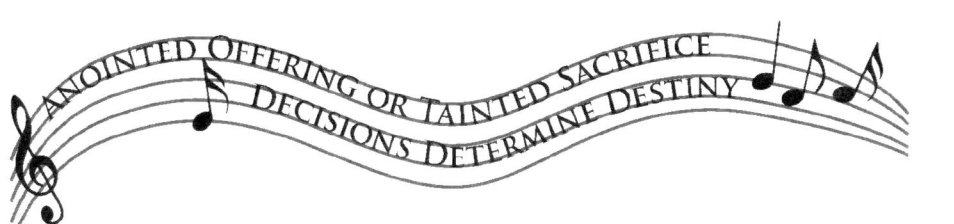

REFERENCES

A. Wilson-Dickson, *The Story of Christian Music* (Batavia, Ill.: Lion, 1992)

Altern Ther Health Medicine 1998 Jan;4(1):75-84

Ballam, Michael. Music and the Mind (Documentation Related to Message)

Collins, Brian, T., The Importance of A=432hz Music

D. P. Hustad, *Jubilate II—Church Music in Worship and Renewal* (Carol Stream, Ill.: Hope Publishing, 1993)

H. M. Best, *Music Through the Eyes of Faith* (San Francisco: Harper, 1993)

Jourdain, Robert. Music, the Brain and Ecstasy. New York: William Morrow and Company, Inc.,1997.

King James Bible

Lundin, Robert W. An Objective Psychology of Music. Malabar: Robert E. Krieger Publishing Company, 1985.

McCraty, Rollin, MA, Barrios Choplin, Bob, PhD, Atkinson, Mike and Tomasino, Dana, BA., "The Effects of Different Types of Music on Mood, Tension and Mental Clarity"

Neverman. "The Affects of Music on the Mind." 3 pp. On-line. Internet. 20 December 1999.

New Unger's Bible Dictionary

O'Donnell, Laurence III, Music and the Brain

Scarantino, Barbara Anne. Music Power Creative Living Through the Joys of Music. New York: Dodd, Mead & Company, 1987.

Storr, Anthony. Music and the Mind. New York: The Free Press, 1992.

Weinberger, N.M. "Threads of Music in the Tapestry of Memory." MuSICA Research Notes 4.1 (Spring 1997): 3pp. On-line. Internet. 13 November 1999.

Wieder, June Leslie book - *The Song of the Spine*

Wikipedia Encyclopedia

Image - copyrighted and courtesy of John Stuart Reid of CymaScope™
Maria Renold's book, *Intervals Scales Tones and the Concert Pitch C=128 Hz*
Kathleen Goss PhD, who works in the Department of Surgery Research – Chicago